MULTICULTURAL READING SERIES

BOOK • 2

by Vivienne Hodges, Ph.D.
& Stuart Margulies, Ph.D.

EDUCATIONAL DESIGN, INC.   EDI 353

ACKNOWLEDGMENTS

The authors wish to thank the following for their kind permission to reprint selections as indicated below.

"Fighting Tennis Champ from Harlem" excerpt from ALWAYS WANTED TO BE SOMBODY, by Althea Gibson and Edward Fitzgerald. Copyright © 1958 by Althea Gibson and Edward Fitzgerald. Reprinted by permission of Harper Collins Publishers, Inc.

TABLE OF CONTENTS

1. The Navajo Code Talkers of World War II 7
   The Native Americans whose coded messages totally baffled the Japanese during World War II.

2. Young Cesar Chavez 13
   The boyhood and young manhood of America's best-known fighter for the rights of migrant farm workers.

3. La Causa 17
   The start of the Farm Workers Union and its early struggles.

4. Music from Motown 23
   Berry Gordy, Jr., the founder of Motown Music—the business that changed American pop music.

5. Fighting Tennis Champ from Harlem 27
   The story of hot-tempered Althea Gibson, America's first African-American tennis champion.

6. Review Questions 31

7. Asian-American TV Anchors 35
   The rise to success of a group of America's best-known TV newscasters.

8. The Power of the Pen 39
   The African-American blast against slavery that terrified the slave owners.

9. The Daily Life of the Aztecs 43
   The incredible achievements of one of America's richest Native American civilizations.

10. Rita Moreno: The Four-Time Winner 47
    The star from Puerto Rico who became the only person to win all four major show-business awards.

11. Famous Amos 53
    Wally Amos, the African-American businessman who became nationally known for a cookie.

12. Review Questions 57

13. The Black Athlete Who Beat the Nazi "Supermen" 61

Jesse Owens, the sickly African-American boy who grew up to become an Olympic star and who defeated Hitler's best athletes.

14. Fiesta in Mexico 67

Mexico's joyous holidays, when people throw off their cares and almost anything goes.

15. The Black Spy Who Saved America 71

James Armistead, the daring slave spy whose information helped win the American Revolution.

16. The Blind Dancer 75

Alicia Alonso, the internationally famous Cuban dancer who prepared for her greatest role when she was blind.

17. Concentration Camps in America 79

The Japanese Americans who were put behind barbed wire in World War II because of racial fears.

18. Review Questions 85

19. King of Salsa 87

Rubén Blades—singer, composer, musician, lawyer, politician, and actor from Panama.

20. Cruelty and Kindness in Florida 93

The true story of a young Spanish soldier who was cruelly treated by one Native American chief and saved by another.

21. El Barrio 97

Daily life in the Puerto Rican section of New York City.

22. The Great Moctezuma 101

The fabulous wealth and power of the last king of the Aztecs, as described by a Spanish soldier who knew him.

23. The Beauty Business of Madame C.J. Walker 107

The poor African-American woman from Louisiana who became a millionaire businesswoman.

24. Review Questions 110

INTRODUCTION

This is a book that will help you read better. It is also a book about some interesting and unusual people.

- You will read about the Native American soldiers whose coded messages baffled the Japanese and helped to win World War II.

- You will read about a young African-American athlete who set three world records when he was so badly injured that he couldn't even bend over.

- You will read about the daring young African-American spy who helped the United States become a free nation—though he himself was a slave.

- You'll read about Cesar Chavez and his lifelong fight for justice and fair treatment of Hispanic migrant workers

This book contains 20 stories. They are about Native Americans, and Americans whose ancestors came here from places as far apart as Africa and Mexico. There are also stories about people from Puerto Rico, Cuba, Panama, Japan, and China.

The authors of this book hope that you will enjoy reading this book about the many different kinds of people in our country and in our world.

OFFICIAL U.S. MARINE CORPS PHOTO (USMC #69889-A)

Two Navajo Indian Code Talkers in the South Pacific during World War II. Marine Corporal Henry Bake, Jr., and Private First Class George H. Kirk are using a portable radio to send and receive coded messages in the Navajo language. They are kneeling in a clearing that they have hacked from the tropical rain forest of Bougainville Island.

1
THE NAVAJO CODE TALKERS OF WORLD WAR II

In 1941, Japan attacked the U.S. fleet at Pearl Harbor in Hawaii and wiped it out. World War II had begun.

Americans fought back. They attacked islands in the Pacific Ocean that were held by the Japanese. But each time the Marines planned an attack, the Japanese learned about it in advance. They learned about it by listening to the radio. American commanders were sending out radio messages to their troops. The messages were in code, but the Japanese always broke the code.

Then the Japanese started hearing something different on the radio. It was a language, but it sounded like no language they had ever heard. They thought it might be a code. But it was a code that their best code-breakers couldn't crack. In fact, the Japanese were listening to messages in a language named *Diné Bizaad*. It is the native language of the Navajo Indians of Arizona and New Mexico.

It all started with Philip Johnston. Johnston was a white man, but he had been raised on the Navajo Reservation. He was one of the few white people who spoke Navajo. At that time, there were no books about the Navajo language. There were no schools for learning Navajo. Most important, there were no Japanese who spoke Navajo. Johnston thought maybe Diné Bizaad could be a new, top-secret code. He told his idea to the Marine Corps.

At first, the Marines were a little doubtful. There were no words for things like bombs and planes in the Navajo language. How could Navajos talk about military matters? But Johnston showed them that it could work. A Navajo speaker was given a message in English. He quickly translated it into the Navajo language and sent the message over the radio to another Navajo speaker. The second man immediately translated the message back into English. When the two English versions were compared, they were exactly the same. And the Navajos handled the message much faster than the regular message senders. The Marines were convinced.

Now came the task of training Navajos for the job. First, the Navajo Tribal Council agreed to the plan. Then the Marines persuaded the first Navajos to sign up. Some of the young men were under 18. Some were so eager to enlist that they lied about their age. By the summer of 1943, there were 191 Navajos in the Marine Corps' code program.

The young Navajos were sent to Marine boot camp. Boot camp is where recruits learn to be Marines. It is tough for all trainees. It was even tougher for the young Navajos. Most of them had never traveled on a train, or even been off their reservation. They had never met anyone like a Marine drill sergeant! The Marines didn't have an easy time with their young recruits either. They weren't used to such calm, patient trainees. Even so, the Navajos learned faster than most recruits. Of the 29 men in the first Navajo platoon, 26 became expert shots.

The Navajos learned how to send messages. They learned how to lay telephone wires and climb telephone poles. Most important, they worked out how to deal with military words and turn them into code words. These words didn't exist in their language. So they used bird names for airplanes. The commanding general became the "war chief." In addition, each letter of the English alphabet was given a simple Navajo word. When the Navajos sent a message, they used these Navajo words in place of English letters. For example, the letter A was the Navajo word for ant. The letter B was bear.

Imagine a Navajo had to send the message: "The General needs a plane." He might begin with the Navajo word for war chief. Then he might turn each letter in "needs a" into its code word in Navajo. "A" would be the Navajo word for ant. He would end his message with a Navajo bird name.

Eight months after the war started, the first Navajo Marines were sent to the Pacific. Pairs of Code Talkers went to different Marine units. Their main job was to send messages over the phone and radio. Of course the Japanese listened in. But they didn't understand a word of what was going on.

GLOSSARY

code A way of writing or sending secret messages so no one can understand them without knowing the secret.

code-breakers People who try to figure out the secret of a code so that they can read the original message.

military matters Matters involving war, defense, the Army, the Navy, the Air Force, etc.

platoon A group of about 30 soldiers or Marines commanded by a lieutenant.

recruit Someone who has just joined a military service.

reservation A special area set aside for Native Americans to live on.

translated Changed from one language into another.

The Japanese got one lucky break. They guessed that the language might be Navajo, and they had taken a Navajo prisoner early in the war. They made him translate a message. But it sounded like nonsense—"Chicken-ant-bear-apple." So they still couldn't break the code.

About 400 Navajo Code Talkers were trained. They took part in every Marine attack of the war. One of their toughest battles was on the island of Iwo Jima. The battle lasted 36 days, and all its messages were handled by Navajo Code Talkers. When the Marines first landed, the most dangerous time, the Navajos sent 800 messages. They made NO mistakes. One of the Marines at Iwo Jima said "They were the kind of guys you'd want to have in your foxhole." An officer said, "Were it not for the Navajos, the Marines would never have taken Iwo Jima."

Even after the war ended, the role of the Navajo Code Talkers was still top secret. Few people knew anything about it. The Code Talkers were ordered to keep silent, and they did so. It's not a secret now, but still some Navajos won't say what they did in the war. They have given their word, and they will keep it.

The Code Talkers fought for their country about 50 years ago, but many are still alive. They have formed their own association with its own special uniform. They march in parades as a unit. They are still heroes, admired and loved by all who see them.

EXERCISES

CONTEXT CLUES

1. One of the Marines at Iwo Jima said of the Navajos, "They were the kind of guys you'd want to have in your <u>foxhole</u>." What do you think the word "foxhole" means in this sentence?

   A) a hole that soldiers dig in the ground to hide in for protection
   B) a place where coyotes and foxes live
   C) a kind of code message
   D) an island with a hole in the middle

CHARACTERS' MOTIVATION

2. Some Navajo Code Talkers still will not talk about what they did in the war. How does the selection explain this?

   A) They are ashamed of what they did.
   B) They promised not to talk, and they are still keeping their promise.
   C) They don't remember what they did.
   D) It is still against the law to talk about it.

COMPARE/CONTRAST

3. How were the Navajo recruits different from other Marine recruits?

   A) The were much bigger and stronger.
   B) They were much older.
   C) They were not as good at shooting.
   D) They were cooler and less excitable.

MAIN IDEA

4. Why was the Navajo language a good code?

   A) It is similar to Japanese.
   B) It is similar to English.
   C) It's not like any language that the Japanese were familiar with.
   D) It's made up of dots and dashes, like Morse Code.

MAKING JUDGMENTS

5. An <u>amphibious</u> landing is one that begins in the water and ends on the land. What code word do you think the Navajos chose to mean "amphibious"?

   A) *ch'ał*, meaning "frog"
   B) *atsá*, meaning "eagle"
   C) *ch'osh*, meaning "insect"
   D) *gahtsoh*, meaning "rabbit"

WRITE ABOUT—

6. Imagine that you met a Navajo Code Talker and could ask him three questions. What three questions would you ask?

2
YOUNG CESAR CHAVEZ

Ask a bunch of Americans to name a famous Mexican-American. Many will say "Cesar Chavez!" For more than 30 years Cesar Chavez has been famous as a fighter for the rights of a special group of farm workers—the farm workers who pick the fruit and vegetables we eat.

Cesar Chavez was born in Arizona. His parents worked there. Cesar's father worked for the Post Office. Then, in the 1930's, the Great Depression hit America. Millions of people lost their jobs. Cesar's father was one of them. Cesar's parents became migrant workers.

A migrant is someone who is always on the move. Migrant workers are the farm workers who pick tomatoes, or avocados, or grapes, or lettuce. Throughout the year, they move to wherever a crop is ripe and pick it.

As migrant workers, the Chavez family had no home. Sometimes they lived in their car. Sometimes they lived in tar paper shacks or tents. Sometimes they slept underneath a highway bridge. Cesar kept changing schools. He attended more than thirty schools. He didn't learn much. In seventh grade, he still had trouble reading. He could hardly write.

Cesar worked even when he was a little kid. He earned a little money for the family. "We used to shine shoes, my brother and I. We would do anything to make a dime. We really hustled."

He learned all about racism. Cesar remembers it very well. He and his brother went to a diner. It had a sign reading "Whites Only." "We didn't know about those things. We didn't understand. So we just went in."

The waitress was with her boyfriend. "I said, 'Two hamburgers please.' The girl said, 'What's the matter, can't you read? Damn dumb Mex.' She and her boyfriend laughed at us. We ran out. Richard cursed them. But I was the one who had spoken to them. I was crying. That laugh rang in my ears for twenty years. It seemed to cut us out of the human race."

Cesar became a rebel. At thet time, every movie house had a special Mexican section. Mexicans and Mexican-Americans were supposed to sit there and nowhere else. Cesar refused to sit in the Mexican section. He sat wherever he wanted to. Many times he was thrown out into the street.

Those were hard years for the migrant farm workers. Sometimes they went on strike. Cesar's father and uncle went on strike too. They wanted to earn more money. But nothing much changed. The farm workers were always on the move. It was hard to build a union. The migrant workers stayed in one place for only about a week. Also, the strikers had no money. Without money, how could they feed their families if they were on strike?

Young Cesar watched and listened. From his father, he learned that life is tough. His mother taught him to hate fighting. She was against violence. She said the children must share what they have.

When Cesar was fifteen, he met a girl named Helen Fabela. They dated for a while. But World War II had just started. Cesar joined the Navy. He was sent to the Pacific. Back home after the war, the first thing he did was to get a job. He became a farm worker. The second thing was to marry Helen.

Cesar and his wife lived in San Jose, California. They lived in a *barrio*, that is, a Hispanic neighborhood. Their barrio was called "Sal Si Puedes." This means "Get out if you can." Nobody wanted to live there, it was so poor.

In Sal Si Puedes, Cesar began his work with the migrant workers.

The story of how Cesar founded the Farm Workers Union is told in the next selection.

GLOSSARY

strike Stopping work and refusing to go back until you get better pay or better job conditions.

union A workers' organization.

EXERCISES

SAME MEANINGS

1. Cesar says that he and his brother <u>really hustled.</u> What has the same meaning as "hustled"?

   A) ran away
   B) studied
   C) worked hard
   D) lived cheaply

SEQUENCE

2. Which of these things happened <u>last</u>?

   A) Cesar dated Helen Fabela.
   B) Cesar became a farm worker.
   C) Cesar settled in Sal Si Puedes.
   D) Cesar's father became a migrant worker.

CAUSE/EFFECT

3. Why did Cesar and Richard run out of the diner?

   A) They didn't have enough money.
   B) They couldn't read.
   C) The diner didn't serve hamburgers.
   D) The waitress made fun of them.

TRUE/FALSE

4. Which is NOT true?

   A) Cesar was born in Mexico.
   B) Cesar joined the Navy.
   C) Cesar's mother was against violence.
   D) Cesar's father was poor.

FIGURATIVE LANGUAGE

5. Cesar said. "That laugh rang in my ears for twenty years." What did he mean?

   A) He needed more money.
   B) He couldn't forget what happened.
   C) He felt happy.
   D) He was angry at his brother.

WRITE ABOUT—

6. Imagine you are a low-paid farm worker at the time Cesar Chavez was a boy. Another worker suggests going on strike for better pay. What would you tell her, and why?

3
LA CAUSA

You read about Cesar Chavez in the last selection. He was a boy then, and had gone through some very tough times. When we left him, he'd just gotten married and moved to San Jose.

In San Jose, Cesar worked in a lumber yard during the day. At night, he worked as a volunteer for a group called the CSO (Community Service Organization). At that time, few of the farm workers could vote. Either they weren't citizens or they weren't registered. The CSO believed that if farm workers could vote, they'd get more power. They might even get better schools for their kids. Cesar traveled up and down the San Joaquin valley. His job was to meet the farm workers. He asked them what they needed and how he could help. He talked about how important it was to vote.

Cesar was shy at first. He hated talking to crowds. But when he did, people would say, "He's wonderful." The farm workers liked and trusted Cesar. He says, "The business of convincing a man is the business of spending time with him. And you have to draw a picture and make it plain. You have to talk facts about things he can see. Theories don't work."

After a while, Cesar left his job in the lumber yard and worked full time for the CSO. But he was unhappy. He didn't think the CSO could solve the farm workers' problems. The farm workers needed a union. So he started one.

Cesar wanted the farm workers to feel the new union belonged to them. One time, a stranger wanted to give the new union $50,000. But Cesar said no. The union should not depend on one man's gift. This made his brother Richard so mad, he almost quit. Still, the union did need money. Cesar gave his own savings. His relatives made gifts to the union. Farm workers gave food and clothing. The union was too poor to pay Cesar. His wife Helen worked to support the whole family.

Cesar wanted more farm workers to join the union. He visited 87 villages and migrant camps. He talked to everyone. He worked 18 hours a day. He got up very early and drove round knocking on doors. He went to the fields. He didn't stop talking.

The farm workers had three big problems. The first was health. The workers had to bend over to pick fruit. Many of them hurt their backs this way. The second problem was jobs. Every harvest, workers were brought into California from Mexico. This took jobs away from Mexican-American farm workers. Pay was the third problem. Farm workers were paid very little. Cesar asked workers what would be a fair wage. He was shocked when they answered "$1.10 an hour." He was aiming for $1.75.

In 1965, the grape pickers went on strike. They wanted higher pay. The great struggle known as La Causa ("The Cause") had begun. After a while, one of the big wine grape growers agreed to raise the pickers' wages to $1.75. The other growers soon followed.

The wine grape pickers had won. But table grape pickers were still on strike. Their growers wouldn't give in. Cesar came up with the idea of a boycott. He asked Americans to stop buying California grapes. In the big cities of the East and Midwest, people did just that. Sales dropped 20 percent. But the strike dragged on. Some strikers wanted to use violence. "A little dynamite. Let's use a little dynamite," they said. But Cesar said no. He did not want La Causa to cost a single life.

He had a better idea: a fast. In 1968 he stopped eating for 25 days. Newspapers all over the country carried the news of his fast. At the end of the fast, Senator Robert Kennedy handed him a piece of bread—his first food in almost a month.

Finally, the table grape growers signed contracts with the union. The contracts said only union members could pick grapes. Cesar called off the boycott. The strike was over. It had lasted five long years.

But the farm workers' struggle wasn't over. Many lettuce pickers had joined a rival union. Cesar was sure the other union was really working with the growers— they didn't care about the pickers. Grape growers started signing with the rival union, too. Suddenly, there was a lot of violence. UFW supporters were attacked. Some were shot. But Cesar and the UFW held on.

Cesar fasted again in 1988. He was protesting the chemicals sprayed on fruits and vegetables. These chemicals can harm the farm workers who pick the crops. They also harm the customers who eat them. This time it was Mrs. Robert Kennedy who gave Cesar the bread which broke his fast.

Cesar Chavez is convinced the union will survive and grow. He is still union president. He's the poorest paid union president in America, by his own choice. A senator once asked him how long it would take to solve the problems of the farm workers. "A lifetime," he replied.

GLOSSARY

fast Going without food.

registered Signed up to be a voter.

theories Ideas that explain something. Theories, even true ones, are often hard to understand.

volunteer Someone who works without pay, because he or she wants to.

EXERCISES

MAIN IDEA

1. This selection tells us—

   A) how the Farm Workers Union got started.
   B) how to grow and sell grapes.
   C) what books Cesar read.
   D) about Cesar's children.

CONTEXT CLUES

2. Which is an example of a <u>boycott</u>?

   A) People stop buying something.
   B) Growers stop growing grapes.
   C) Farm workers refuse to pick grapes.
   D) Farm owners pay low wages.

CHARACTER'S MOTIVES

3. Why did Cesar Chavez go on fasts?

   A) He wasn't hungry.
   B) He wanted to draw attention to the farm workers' problems.
   C) He wanted to lose weight.
   D) He didn't like the food in California.

WORD MEANINGS

4. Which is an example of a strike?

   A) When a car is driven too quickly.
   B) When people won't go to work.
   C) When someone refuses to eat.
   D) When a person prays for a whole day.

SEQUENCE

5. Which came first?

    A) Cesar Chavez broke his first fast.
    B) The grape boycott was called off.
    C) The grape-pickers went on strike.
    D) Cesar Chavez formed the Farm Workers Union.

CHARACTER'S MOTIVES

6. Why was Chavez against the use of dynamite?

    A) Dynamite is expensive.
    B) Dynamite is hard to use.
    C) He didn't want to harm the grapes.
    D) He didn't want anyone to get hurt.

WRITE ABOUT—

7. Imagine that you belong to the Farm Workers Union. You are trying to persuade supermarket shoppers not to buy grapes from Tedesco Farms. Tedesco is a grower that treats its workers badly. One slogan you have thought of is: "HELP THE PICKERS. DON'T BUY TEDESCO GRAPES." Can you make up two more?

THE SUPREMES

Diana Ross (center) and The Supremes, Berry Gordy's most successful Motown singing group.

4
MUSIC FROM MOTOWN

African-American singers are famous today. So are African-American song-writers. They're top of the pops. But back in 1959, things were different.

Berry Gordon, Jr., was a young African-American songwriter. He was having a hard time. No one listened to his songs. Record companies wouldn't record his music. Then a close friend named Smokey Robinson gave Berry some good advice: "Start your own company!"

Berry took the advice. He gave himself a catchy new name, Berry Gordy. And he started his own record company. Black musicians came from all over the U.S. Thousands of singers and musicians came to work with Berry. He bought an old brownstone house in Detroit for his company.

Detroit is the center of the car and motor industry. Its nickname is "Motown." Berry called his company "Motown Music." People began to call the music itself "Motown." That's how Motown music was born.

Berry's first musicians were his friends. They were like one big family. Berry was the "father." He set up a department for young girl singers. They learned how to dress, use make-up, and style their hair.

Motown's sound was different. It had a strong beat. The songs had catchy words. They were sung by a lead singer with a few backup singers. Some of the groups were very smooth. There were the Temptations, the Marvelettes, and many more. Berry's friend Smokey Robinson put together one of the top groups—Smokey Robinson and the Miracles.

Motown singers didn't just sing their songs. They created acts. Motown groups had dancing and waving as well as singing. Most songs were about teenage love. The Four Tops sang, "Baby, I need your loving." America's teenagers hummed along with them.

In 1961, Gordy heard an eleven-year-old singer and piano player. His name was Steveland Morris. Gordy's sister suggested a new name—"Little Stevie Wonder." In those days, people thought Stevie was too young to make records. Stevie Wonder is world famous now.

Smokey Robinson also helped discover new stars. A young girl lived in Smokey's house. She wanted to be a singer. Her name was Diane Ross. Smokey liked her singing. So did Berry. Diane made a record on the Motown label. By 1964 Diana Ross and the Supremes were heard everywhere. They were at the top of the charts.

Motown's best years were 1965 and 1966. Berry's company turned out hit song after hit song. Motown was one of the most successful record companies in America. Everyone, black and white, loved the music. Everyone listened and danced to the Motown sound.

But by 1970, it looked as if Motown was almost finished. The best artists left. Diana Ross left. Stevie Wonder changed to another record company. One of Motown's last famous groups was the Jackson Five. But they, too, left in 1974. There was a lot of bad feeling. Some backup singers were jealous of the big stars. Some musicians felt Berry had cheated them.

Then, in the 1980's, Motown made a comeback. Its hit records were released again. Motown music was used in exercise classes. Motown records were played over the radio again.

Motown has stopped making new music. But America still listens to its songs.

GLOSSARY

catchy Clever and easy to remember.

charts Lists of hit records.

EXERCISES

CHARACTER DESCRIPTION

1. What kind of a person was Berry Gordy?

   A) lazy
   B) stupid
   C) smart
   D) weak

SENTENCE COMPLETION

2. Motown music was usually about teenage love. Its songs were good to dance to. They were usually sung by _____ that contained a solo singer and a few backup singers.

   A) dance bands
   B) groups
   C) solo singers
   D) low voices

MULTIPLE MEANINGS

3. The selection says that the Motown sound has a <u>strong beat</u>. This means that—

   A) it is loud.
   B) it has a strong rhythm.
   C) it has good words.
   D) it makes you cry.

SUPPORTING DETAILS

4. How did Smokey Robinson meet Diane Ross?

   A) They were neighbors.
   B) They worked for a car company.
   C) They were both friends of Berry Gordy.
   D) They were relatives.

CAUSE/EFFECT

5. Why did Motown stop making new records?

   A) It ran out of money.
   B) Its best singers left.
   C) Berry Gordy moved to another country.
   D) Its offices burned down.

WRITE ABOUT—

6. You and four friends have decided to form a singing group like the Motown groups. You will be the lead singer. What will you name your group? What will you call yourself? (You can change your name like Berry Gordon, Diane Ross, and Steveland Morris did.)

5
FIGHTING TENNIS CHAMP FROM HARLEM

Althea Gibson was a street kid from Harlem who became the best female tennis player in the world. She was the first great African-American tennis player. She told her life story in a book called Always Wanted to be Somebody. Here is part of her story, in her own words:.

The only thing I really liked to do was play ball. Basketball was my favorite, but any kind of ball would do. I guess the main reason why I hated to go to school was because I couldn't see any point in wasting all that time that I could be spending shooting baskets in the playground . . . .

I know it sounds indelicate coming from a girl, but I could fight, too. Daddy taught me the moves, and I had the right temperament for it. I was tough, I wasn't afraid of anybody, not even him . . . .

There was a musician fellow, Buddy Walker, . . . watching me play paddle tennis one day, when he suddenly got the idea that I might be able to play regular tennis just as well if I got the chance. So, out of the kindness of his heart, he bought me a couple of secondhand tennis rackets for five dollars apiece and started me out hitting balls against the wall on the handball courts at Morris Park.

Buddy got very excited about how well I hit the ball. [He arranged for Althea to take lessons at a tennis club.] . . . and I began to learn something about the game of tennis. I already knew <u>how</u> to hit the ball but I didn't know <u>why</u>. He taught me some footwork and some court strategy, and along with that he also tried to help me improve my personal ways. He didn't like my arrogant attitude and tried to show me why I should change.

I don't think he got too far in that department; my mind was set pretty strong. I was willing to do what he said about tennis, but I figured what I did away from the courts was none of his business. I wasn't exactly ready to start studying how to be a fine lady . . .

I really wasn't the tennis type. But the polite manners of the game, that seemed so silly to me at first, gradually began to appeal to me. So did the pretty white clothes. I had trouble as a competitor because I kept wanting to fight the other player every time I started to lose a match. But I could see that certain things were expected . . .

After a while I began to understand that you could walk out on the court like a lady, all dressed up in immaculate white, be polite to everybody, and still play like a tiger and beat the liver and lights out of the ball . . . .

I'm ashamed to say I was still living pretty wild. I was supposed to be looking for a job but I didn't look very hard because I was too busy playing tennis in the daytime and having fun at night. The hardest work I did, aside from practicing tennis, was to report to the Welfare ladies once a week, tell them how I was getting along, and pick up my allowance. Then I would celebrate by spending the whole day in the movies and filling myself up with a lot of cheap food.

But I guess it would have been too much to expect me to change completely right away. Actually, I realize now that every day I played tennis and got more interested in the game I was changing a little bit. I just wasn't aware of it.

———————————

Althea Gibson went on to become one of the game's truly great players. She won both the American and British championships in1957 and 1958, and she also won the British doubles titles three years in a row.

GLOSSARY

arrogant   Stuck-up and proud.

immaculate   Spotlessly clean.

indelicate   Not modest; coarse and rude.

liver and lights   Liver and lungs. "Beating the liver and lights out of the ball" means "hitting the ball really hard."

temperament   Personality; attitude

EXCERCISES

FIGURATIVE LANGUAGE

1. Althea says, "Buddy didn't like my arrogant attitude and tried to show me why I should change. I don't think he <u>got too far in that department</u>."

   When she says that she doesn't think Buddy "got too far in that department," she means—

   A) he didn't do well at work.
   B) he couldn't change her.
   C) he taught her how to play tennis.
   D) he got lost.

MAIN IDEA

2. What is the main idea of this selection?

   A) Althea had to learn how to be a tennis star.
   B) Althea liked wearing white tennis clothes.
   C) Althea's friend, Buddy, was a musician.
   D) Althea lived in Harlem.

SEQUENCE

3. What happened first?
   A) Althea learned to play tennis.
   B) Althea got her welfare check.
   C) Althea was given a tennis racket.
   D) Althea played basketball.

COMPARE/ CONTRAST

4. Althea changed when she began to play serious tennis. Which sentence describes the old Althea?

   A) She wore white tennis clothes.
   B) She was very polite to everybody.
   C) She wanted to fight her opponents.
   D) She behaved like a lady on the tennis court.

CAUSE/ EFFECT

5. Why did Althea hate school?

   A) She was a poor student.
   B) She wanted to play basketball instead.
   C) She was always getting into fights.
   D) She wanted to play tennis instead.

WRITE ABOUT—

6. Althea Gibson had to learrn to control her temper before she became a sports star. If you became a sports star, what would you change about yourself?

6
REVIEW QUESTIONS

I. CROSSWORD

CLUES ACROSS

1. Motown's home town.
4. First name of one of Motown's greatest stars, _____ Ross.
5. Code word for the letter "A" used by Navajo Code Talkers.
6. Long fight between grape growers and pickers, known as La _____.

CLUES DOWN

2. Althea's game.
3. Vegetable picked by Chavez family.

II. WHO IS SPEAKING?

7. "I'm no lady. But I'm getting better."

   "Why would anyone want to be in school when they could be playing ball?"

   "Maybe these pretty white clothes aren't so bad after all."

   A) Diana Ross
   B) Berry Gordy
   C) Helen Chavez
   D) Althea Gibson

8. "We would do almost anything to make a dime. We really hustled."

   "You have to talk facts with people. Theories don't work."

   "La Causa will not cost a single life."

   A) a Navajo Code Talker
   B) Berry Gordy
   C) Cesar Chavez
   D) Smokey Robinson

9. "War chief needs an eagle."

   "I cannot talk. I have given my word."

   "Yes sir, I turned 18 last month. I'm plenty old enough to be a Marine."

   A) a Navajo Code Talker
   B) Japanese soldier
   C) Little Stevie Wonder
   D) Althea Gibson

10. "Listen, Berry! Start your own company."

    "She's my neighbor. Wait till you hear this little girl sing!"

    "Meet my very own group, The Miracles."

    A) Diana Ross
    B) Smokey Robinson
    C) Richard Chavez
    D) Althea Gibson

III. MISSING PERSONS

In each of these passages a person's first name is hidden. For example, look at this passage:

I'm glad **I, an a**mateur singer, got discovered by Smokey Robinson.

The name of **Diana** Ross is hidden. The meaning of the whole passage also gives you a clue to the name.

Now see if you can find the first names hidden in these two sentences. And remember, the meaning of each sentence is also a clue about who the person is.

11. Heal the athlete fast, for she has a big game tomorrow. _____

12. He races around talking to the grape pickers. _____

CONNIE CHUNG

Newscaster Connie Chung, one of the earliest and most successful Asian-American TV anchors.

7
ASIAN-AMERICAN TV ANCHORS

One of the top jobs on TV is the job of anchor on a news program. Anchors are the reporters you see in the TV studios. They control the news program and read the main stories. Twenty years ago, nearly all the anchors were men. Today, many are women. A surprisingly large number are Asian-American women.

None of these women started off as anchors. At first, they worked behind the scenes. Most started at the bottom. They got coffee. They did odd jobs. Some worked as volunteers for no pay. Connie Chung, who became a TV anchor, says, "I was a schlep [fetcher and carrier] like everyone else."

Then, in the 1970's, one or two Asian faces appeared on TV. They had been promoted to the job of reporter. This was a big event for many Asian-American women. Wendy Tokuda, who became a TV reporter herself, remembers seeing Barbara Tanabe on TV. "The whole family rushed to the television set."

The movement to put Asian-American reporters onto the TV screen started in San Francisco. San Francisco has one of the largest populations of Asian Americans in the country. It was logical that the first Asian-American reporters should be on San Francisco TV. By 1974, every San Francisco TV station had an Asian-American reporter. It was usually a woman.

The new reporters had a lot to learn. News reporting is a tough job. Reporters have to interview people. They have to know what is important. They must speak well. They must write clearly. And everything must be ready by news time at 6 P.M. or 11 P.M.

The women had one big problem. They had to be tough. Asian-American women in particular are taught to be polite. They are taught to stay out of other people's business. Now they had to learn to be assertive. Chicago anchor Linda Yu says the work really changed her. "People won't believe today that this person that I am used to barely speak above a whisper, always went to the back of the line."

Their worst problems were with the camera crews. Crew members were usually older white men. They didn't like taking orders from young Asian-American women. So Connie and Kaity, Barbara and Wendy had to learn how to get the crews to work with them. There were many fights and bad moments along the way.

Some women left TV reporting. Genny Lim was working for CBS News. She wrote a story about Dennis Banks, a Native American leader. But she says "CBS wouldn't run it. They said the pieces were too sympathetic to Indians." So she resigned.

Linda Shen used to be a TV reporter, too. She interviewed a black welfare mother. The woman had lost everything in a fire. Later, Linda's boss asked her, "Did you get her to cry on camera?" Linda was disgusted with him. She quit.

But most of the reporters stayed on. And after a while, some Asian-American reporters were promoted to the top spot—the job of news anchor. Wendy Tokuda and Connie Chung were two of the early ones. By 1985, there were Asian-American anchor women in America's four largest cities.

Asian-American women used to have an "image" problem. For years, they were not shown as real people. In movies and TV, they were shown as fragile China Dolls or as wicked Dragon Ladies. No more. They have shown that they are hard-working, serious professionals. America respects them.

GLOSSARY

assertive   Confident and willing to speak up for yourself.

fragile   Easily broken; delicate.

populations   Numbers of people.

EXERCISES

MAIN IDEA

1. The main idea of this selection is that—

   A) news stories must be ready by 6 PM.
   B) few Asian-American men have TV jobs.
   C) many news reporters are now Asian-American women.
   D) camera crews treated Asian-American women poorly.

MAKING JUDGMENTS

2. News reporters like their jobs because—

   A) they never get fired.
   B) they don't have to work very hard.
   C) everyone is always helpful.
   D) the work is exciting.

FIGURATIVE LANGUAGE

3. The selection says that Asian-Americans worked <u>behind the scenes</u> at first. This means that—

   A) they did not appear on camera.
   B) they moved furniture around.
   C) they read the news on TV.
   D) they worked at home.

CHARACTERS' MOTIVATION

4. Some Asian-American reporters quit their jobs because—

   A) they had to start at the bottom.
   B) they did not want to be unfair or cruel.
   C) men were doing the most exciting work.
   D) the pay is bad.

WORD MEANING

5. The selection says Asian-American women had an <u>image problem.</u> This means—

   A) people didn't like the way they looked.
   B) people were cruel to them.
   C) people saw them as types, not as individual human beings.
   D) people didn't like their food.

WRITE ABOUT—

6. Imagine you are a TV reporter interviewing one of the women mentioned in the selection. Think of three questions you would like to ask this woman. Try to make your questions interesting, as a real reporter would.

8
THE POWER OF
THE PEN

"I ask you, had you not rather be killed than to be a slave to a tyrant? Believe this, that it is no more harm for you to kill a man who is trying to kill you than it is for you to take a drink of water when thirsty."

These words of fire were written to the enslaved black people of the South in 1829. The author was a man that almost nobody had heard of—a seller of used clothes in Boston. But his words made him instantly famous. His name was David Walker, and he was the first African American to call for his enslaved brothers and sisters to throw off their chains and rise up against slavery.

David Walker was an unusual man. He was born in the South, in the state of North Carolina. But unlike most African American children in the South, he was not born into slavery. He was one of the very few Southern blacks who were born free.

As a young man, David traveled through the Southern States. He was horrified to see how his people were treated. He finally left the South and moved North, where slavery was against the law. In Boston, he opened a store where he sold used clothes. But he couldn't forget what he had seen. He wanted his people to be free like him.

At that time, many white Americans thought slavery was wrong. Some of them spoke out and wrote against it. But in the early days of the movement against slavery, most of these people wanted to end slavery by shipping African Americans back to Africa. Few of them were exciting writers, and whatever they wrote was addressed only to other white people.

David Walker was different. He felt that sending blacks to Africa was a trick. He believed it was meant to get rid of the bravest and most intelligent blacks who might be leaders of their people. Most African Americans would still be in slavery. Without possible leaders, they would be easier to manage.

Walker wanted his people to fight for their freedom here in America. It was their own country. They had earned it. He declared: "The greatest riches in America have risen from our blood and tears."

In 1829, Walker wrote a paper that he named *Walker's Appeal to the Colored Citizens of the World*. He asked African Americans this question: Why should they be enslaved? Black people knew slavery was wrong. Therefore they must fight for their freedom. The *Appeal* ended with a warning to white Americans:

"You may do your best to keep us in wretchedness and misery, to enrich you and your children, but God will deliver us from under you. And woe, woe will be to you if we have to obtain our freedom by fighting."

The *Appeal* startled the country. Thousands of people were stirred by Walker's words. Within a year, the *Appeal* was reprinted three times.

Southern slave owners were furious. They didn't want any trouble with their slaves. They certainly didn't want slaves to read Walker's *Appeal*. So the slave owners burned every copy they could find. They waited for a boat to arrive in a port. Then they searched the sailors to make sure they weren't hiding the *Appeal*. If they found any copies of the paper, they burned it.

The slave owners threatened to kill Walker. He replied: "I will stand my ground." But shortly after this, he disappeared. No one ever saw him alive again.

David Walker didn't use a gun. His weapon was the printed word, and his message helped change history. Other people began to call for the total ending of the slavery system. Great African-American speakers and writers like Frederick Douglass and Sojourner Truth moved thousands with their words and with the stories of their lives. The editor William Lloyd Garrison started a newspaper, *The Liberator*, devoted to ending slavery. The movement against slavery grew and grew.

In 1861 the United States plunged into a Civil War. In that war, black people gave their answer to Walker's *Appeal*. More than 180,000 black soldiers joined the Union army. They helped destroy the system that David Walker had written against more than thirty years before.

GLOSSARY

enslaved Put into slavery.

tyrant A cruel ruler.

wretchedness Miserable conditions.

EXERCISES

WORD MEANINGS

1. The selection says that Walker's *Appeal* <u>stirred</u> thousands of Americans.

   Which word has the same meaning as "stirred?"

   A) bored
   B) excited
   C) amused
   D) annoyed

OUTLINING

2. Look at this outline of events in the selection.

   I. David Walker traveled around the South.
   II. David Walker wrote his *Appeal*.
   III. ———————————
   IV. David Walker disappeared.

   What belongs in the missing part of this outline?

   A) David Walker was born in the South.
   B) David Walker moved to Boston.
   C) David Walker said he would stand his ground.
   D) David Walker opened a used clothing store.

MAKING JUDGMENTS

3. David Walker was against sending black people back to Africa. What <u>two</u> of the following reasons did he have for feeling this way?

   A) He thought that it would cost too much.
   B) He though that it was a plot to get rid of possible black leaders.
   C) He thought that Africa was a terrible place.
   D) He thought that black people had earned the right to consider America their home.

DRAWING CONCLUSIONS

4. What happened to David Walker? The selection implies that—

   A) his enemies killed him.
   B) he went to Africa.
   C) he lived to be an old man.
   D) he returned to the South.

FACT/OPINION

5. Which of the following statements is an opinion, not a fact?

   A) David Walker was one of the very few Southern blacks who was born free.
   B) Believe this, that it is no more harm for you to kill a man who is trying to kill you than it is for you to take a drink of water when thirsty.
   C) Walker disappeared, and no one ever saw him alive again.
   D) Walker left the South and moved North, where slavery was against the law.

WRITE ABOUT—

6. Imagine that you are a slave in the South in 1829. You read a copy of David Walker's *Appeal.* What is your reaction? Which part of Walker's *Appeal* means the most to you?

9
THE DAILY LIFE OF THE AZTECS

In 1519, a Spanish soldier named Cortés landed on the shores of Mexico. He had about 500 soldiers with him. In two years, these few men conquered and destroyed one of the world's great civilizations, the civilization of the Aztec Indians.

Aztec civilization was strange to the Spanish. It seems just as strange to us today. The Aztecs had a bloody, cruel religion. Every year they killed thousands of captives to feed their gods. But they were also an intelligent, artistic people who loved poetry and flowers. In some ways, they were more civilized than the Spanish who conquered them.

The chief Aztec city stood where Mexico City stands today. It was built on several islands in a lake. This island city was a crowded place. Thousands of people lived there, and they all had to be fed. Every inch of soil was used to grow food.

But the Aztec farmers needed still more soil. They found it in an strange place. They scraped it from the bottom of the lake. This lake soil was placed on floating rafts made of reeds and roots. The farmers then grew food on the rafts. The lake was covered with these tiny floating farms. each farmer steered his farm around with a long pole.

The Aztecs were skilled farmers. They were the first to grow some of our favorite foods. Chocolate and cocoa came from the cacao beans they grew. They also grew corn, wild bananas, tomatoes, and beans. A favorite vegetable was the root of a mountain plant that also had a beautiful flower. Today, we grow this plant just for its flowers. It is called the dahlia. It is one of the most common flowers in our flower shops.

One of the most important Aztec crops was a plant called the maguey. The Aztecs found many uses for this plant. They drank juice pressed from its long, thick leaves. They ate its roots. They wrote on a kind of paper made from it. Thread, rope, and cloth sandals were made from stringy fibers in the leaves.

The edges of the maguey leaf have sharp thorns. Even these were used. The Aztecs made pins and needles from them. The leaves themselves were used in the walls and roofs of their houses.

The Aztecs knew how to stay healthy. The lake water was no good for drinking. So the Aztecs built an aqueduct to bring in good drinking water. This clean water filled their fountains all over the city. The Aztecs were just as careful about human waste. Boats were tied at central points in the city. The boats were used as toilets. The waste products weren't wasted! Urine was used to help dye cloth. Excrement was used as a fertilizer.

The Aztecs realized that a clean city is a healthy city. Europeans of the time didn't know this. European cities were filthy. After the Spanish conquest, the Aztec floating toilets were no longer used. The Aztec cities became dirty and unhealthy. Thousands died from disease.

There were many different kinds of Aztec money. Gold dust and pieces of tin were money. So were bags of chocolate beans. The nearby town of Tabasco sent a tribute of 10 tons of chocolate beans to the Aztec king. The king and his chiefs drank it all themselves! The Spanish invaders first drank chocolate in Mexico. It tasted bitter and strange, since the Aztecs didn't always sweeten it. Later, in Europe, the Dutch added sugar. Chocolate became a big hit. By 1700, the cities of Europe were filled with chocolate shops.

The Aztecs were great artists. They made gold and silver ornaments with great skill. The Spanish thought they were finer than anything in Europe. When Cortés landed at Vera Cruz, King Moctezuma sent him fabulous gifts. A soldier described two huge plates, one gold and one silver. He said they were as large as carriage wheels. The Spaniards thought the gold plate was worth over a million dollars.

The Aztecs wrote in pictures. Aztec artists recorded laws, legends, and rituals on paper made from the maguey plant. There were thousands of these Aztec "books" when the Spanish invaded Mexico. The Spanish burned nearly all of them. To the Spaniards, they were the work of people who worshiped devils. And so, there is a lot we can never know about the marvelous civilization of the Aztecs.

The ruler of the Aztecs was named Moctezuma. In another selection in this book, you will find out what he was like and read about about his incredible power and wealth.

GLOSSARY

aqueduct A long pipe that carries water to a city from a mountain lake.

civilization An advanced and complex way of life.

conquered Beaten in war.

excrement Waste matter from the bowels.

rituals Ways of performing religious acts.

EXERCISES

VOCABULARY DEVELOPMENT

1. The Aztecs built a long water pipe to bring clean water to their capital city.

   Which word in the selection has the same meaning as "long water pipe"?

   A) organ
   B) drain
   C) aqueduct
   D) fountain

REFERENCE

2. Which would tell you more about the Aztec religion?

   A) an atlas
   B) an encyclopedia
   C) an almanac
   D) a dictionary

COMPARE/ CONTRAST

3. Which is false?

   A) The Aztecs wrote picture books.
   B) The Spanish wanted a lot of gold.
   C) The Aztecs used clean water.
   D) European cities at the time of Cortés were very clean.

VOCABULARY DEVELOPMENT

4. The town of Tabasco sent a <u>tribute</u> to King Moctezuma.

   From your reading of the selection, what do you think the word *tribute* could mean?

   A) payments and gifts made by a weak country to a strong one
   B) messages of love and friendship
   C) poison
   D) orders and commands that have to be obeyed

USE OF IDIOM

6. Chocolate was a <u>big hit</u> in Europe. This means the people in Europe—

    A) never heard of chocolate.
    B) liked chocolate a lot.
    C) used chocolate as a medicine.
    D) hated chocolate.

WRITE ABOUT—

7. Suppose you are a soldier with Cortés. Make a list of three things that you admire about the Aztecs or the Aztec way of life. Write a sentence about each item on the list telling why you admire it.

10
RITA MORENO: THE FOUR-TIME WINNER

Rita Moreno is an entertainer. And what an entertainer! She makes sparks fly. She's an actor, a singer, and above all, a dancer. She has appeared in movies, on records, on TV, and in Broadway plays. She has had one of the most extraordinary careers in the history of American entertainment.

Rita was born Rosa Dolores Alverio in Puerto Rico in 1931. When she was just a baby, her parents divorced. Her mother went to New York City to find work. Little Rita had to stay behind in Puerto Rico with other family members. For four lonely years, Mrs. Alverio worked as a seamstress. Finally she earned enough money to bring Rosita—little Rosa— to America.

Rosita took dance lessons in New York. Quickly, she found a job—in the toy department of Macy's. But she wasn't a salesperson. Children visiting Macy's Toy Department saw little Rosita, all dressed up, singing and dancing. A few years later, when she was thirteen, Rosita won a role on Broadway. But the show closed after just one week.

Rosita Moreno—Moreno was her stepfather's last name—moved on to Hollywood. In 1950, she appeared in her first film. Other small parts followed. One time she was cast in a movie that had some key scenes in a swimming pool. Rosita wanted the job a lot. The movie director asked, "Can you swim?" "Sure," she said. It was a lie. She almost drowned.

In Hollywood, Rosita shortened her first name to Rita. After a year of bit parts in films, she was sure she had it made. She was sure she was going to be the biggest, hottest star that ever happened. But then the film studio said she was fired. Rita was shattered. Her dreams had come to nothing.

Then, after a few bad years, Rita got a break. She landed a part in a big movie. It was a hit musical, *The King and I*. Rita played the key role of Tuptim, the King's young wife, who tries to run away with her lover. A famous dance director, Jerome Robbins, wrote the dance steps for the movie. When Robbins began to work on a new Broadway musical that featured Puerto Rican kids in New York, he remembered Rita. Unfortunately, she was busy. She couldn't play *West Side Story* on Broadway— and it turned out to be one of the greatest musical shows of all time. But when Robbins cast the movie version, Rita was ready.

RITA MORENO

Rita Moreno, the only performer in history to win all four top American awards in the entertainment field— the Oscar, the Emmy. the Tony, and the Grammy.

West Side Story was about teenage gangs in New York City. Rita played the wild, glamorous Anita. Anita's boyfriend was the leader of the boys' gang, and Anita led the girls. Her dancing was fast and sexy. She swung her hips like crazy. Her clothes were bright and daring. She almost stole the show. The movie won ten Oscars, including one for Rita as Best Supporting Actress. And it had a big impact on Latin dance styles.

After *West Side Story,* Rita's career took off. In the 1970's, she was a regular on TV. She starred in a children's TV show, *The Electric Company.* She also had guest appearances on other shows. She appeared on the top-rated detective show, *The Rockford Files,* and with the wildly popular puppets of *The Muppet Show.* She was so good that she won two Emmys, one for each of these roles. She also picked up a Grammy award for the *Electric Company* record album.

Next, Rita played a third-rate singer named Googie Gomez in a Broadway comedy hit, *The Ritz.* She spoke with an exaggerated Spanish accent. *The Ritz* made fun of the phony Hispanics you see in so many TV shows and Hollywood movies. Rita got a big kick out of playing the part. *The Ritz* won Rita a Tony, the Broadway equivalent of an Oscar.

Rita Moreno has won an Oscar, a Tony, a Grammy, and <u>two</u> Emmys! She had set an entertainment record. No one else in entertainment history has won all four awards.

GLOSSARY

bit parts Small parts in a show or a movie.

Broadway The theater district of New York City

Emmy The TV equivalent of an Oscar.

equivalent Something that is equal to something else, or almost the same as something else.

exaggerated Bigger than in real life, or overdone.

Grammy The record industry equivalent of an Oscar.

Macy's A large and famous department store in New York.

Oscar The yearly Academy Award for the best movie and movie performances.

seamstress A woman who sews clothing.

Tony The Broadway equivalent of an Oscar.

EXERCISES

FIGURATIVE LANGUAGE

1. The selection says that Rita Moreno <u>makes sparks fly</u>. This means that Rita—

    A) sweats when she dances.
    B) is a very exciting entertainer.
    C) dances the fire dance.
    D) takes a lot of risks.

OUTLINING

2. What belongs in the missing part of this outline?

    I. Rita tries to swim in a movie.
    II. Rita plays a king's wife.
    III. ....
    IV. Rita appears on TV in the <u>Electric Company</u>.

    A) Rita changes her name.
    B) Rita stars in <u>The Ritz</u> on Broadway.
    C) Rita sings and dances in Macy's.
    D) Rita plays the gang leader, Anita.

FACT/OPINION

3. Which of these statements is a fact, not an opinion?

    A) Rita makes sparks fly as an entertainer.
    B) Rita's career has been extraordinary.
    C) Rita stole the show.
    D) Rita learned to dance in New York.

OPPOSITE MEANINGS

4. Rita was <u>shattered</u> when the studio fired her. What is the opposite of "shattered?"

   A) broken
   B) thrilled
   C) upset
   D) amused

CAUSE/EFFECT

5. Why was Rita hired to play Anita in the movie version of *West Side Story*?

   A) She was a famous dancer.
   B) The dance director remembered her.
   C) She had been a big hit in *The Ritz*.
   D) She needed the job.

WRITE ABOUT—

6. Which of Rita Moreno's famous performances would you most like to see? Why did you choose this performance?

11
FAMOUS AMOS

Have you ever eaten Famous Amos cookies? They're full of chocolate chips. They taste really good! The cookies are the creation of Wallace Amos, the African-American businessman whose picture is on the cookie package. Wally is one of the most successful businessmen in the country. His story shows what can happen if you have intelligence, skill, and luck.

Wally Amos didn't start out as a professional cookie baker. He was a talent agent in New York. Talent agents have an interesting job. They work with actors, musicians, dancers, and writers. Wally had some some really big clients. He worked with the Supremes, Sam Cooke, the Temptations, and The Rolling Stones.

Talent agents get jobs for their clients. But they do a lot more than this. They help clients with their acts. They decide which cities their clients should tour. Some agents must be money experts, too. Big stars often want their agents to look after their money. Agents get a lot of business experience in many different areas.

How did Wally get around to making cookies? Well, when he was twelve, his parents split up. He was sent to live with his aunt in New York City. Aunt Della baked the most delicious—you guessed it—chocolate chip cookies. For years, Wally used Aunt Della's recipe to bake chocolate chip cookies for friends. One day, in 1974, a friend suggested he should sell them.

Wally liked the idea. After all, he had good business skills. He knew how to shape a product to make it successful. He got on well with people. He had a great business idea—opening small shops that would do nothing but sell his cookies. And, most important, he had a great recipe. So Wally Amos became the talent agent for a cookie.

He planned things carefully. First he decided what he needed—food mixers, kitchen tables, cookie ovens. Then, he picked the best spot to open his first cookie store. Next, he went to a group of businessmen. He showed them his plans and asked them to lend him money to get started. They agreed. Famous Amos Chocolate Chip Cookies were on their way.

In 1975, Wally's first store opened. It was an immediate success. Within a year, his factory was baking 6,000 pounds of cookies a day. They were sold in Famous Amos stores across America. After a while, even supermarkets were selling them.

Wallace Amos is proud that he has made his name famous. He has always believed in himself. He reckons that's why he is a success. He knew what he wanted to do. He believed he could do it. He set himself a goal. And he didn't stop until he reached it.

GLOSSARY

clients People who use the services of a professional.

EXERCISES

SEQUENCE

1. Which came first?

   A) Wallace got jobs for musicians.
   B) Wallace ate Aunt Della's cookies.
   C) Wallace built his own factory.
   D) Wallace opened his own cookie store.

OPPOSITE MEANINGS

2. Wallace Amos is <u>proud of his success</u>. Which sentence has the opposite meaning?

   A) Wallace thinks his work is excellent.
   B) Wallace is ashamed of his achievement.
   C) Wallace is funny.
   D) Wallace is helpful.

MAKING JUDGMENTS

3. The author has described a talent agent's job. Which of these things would a talent agent NOT do?

   A) teach singers what to wear
   B) help the stars look after their money
   C) find parts for actors
   D) sing in a rock band

WRITE ABOUT—

4. You are making a TV ad for a brand of fudge brownies called Granny Mudge's Fudge Brownies. The ad shows two people eating the brownies. A group is singing about how good the brownies are. Write a one-line slogan for the announcer to say at the end of the song.

12
REVIEW QUESTIONS

I. CROSSWORD

CLUES ACROSS

1. David Walker wrote a powerful one.
2. Where you can see an Asian-American anchor.
4. You'd like it if Wally Amos made one of these for you.

CLUES DOWN

1. They used to be the rulers of Mexico.
3. Rita Moreno's real first name.

II. MAP

Here is a map of the United States. There are four places marked on the map. Each place is connected with someone in the selections you've just read. Match the person or people with the place.

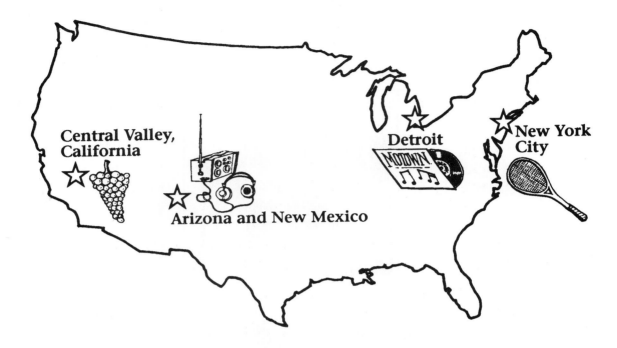

5. ARIZONA AND NEW MEXICO

   A) Rita Moreno
   B) Cesar Chavez
   C) Navajo code talkers
   D) Wallace Amos

6. NEW YORK CITY

   A) Diana Ross
   B) Althea Gibson
   C) David Walker
   D) Navajo Code Talkers

7. DETROIT

   A) Althea Gibson
   B) David Walker
   C) Wallace Amos
   D) Diana Ross

8. CALIFORNIA

   A) Navajo Code Talkers
   B) Asian-American anchors
   C) Cesar Chavez and the grape pickers
   D) The Aztecs

III. MOVIES AND MUSIC

9. What do *West Side Story*, *The King and I,* and *The Muppet Show* have in common?

   A) They all took place in Mexico.
   B) Rita Moreno acted in all three of them.
   C) Each one was about a famous Aztec.
   D) They were songs about the California grape pickers.

10. If you heard an old record of The Supremes, you'd be listening to

   A) Rita Moreno in West Side Story
   B) jazz
   C) the blues
   D) Motown Music

11. What do Berry Gordy and Wallace Amos have in common?

   A) They were both musicians.
   B) They both worked in Detroit.
   C) They both worked with the Supremes and the Temptations.
   D) They both lost money in the stock market.

IV ODD ONE OUT or WHO DOESN'T BELONG?

12. All these people lived and worked in cities EXCEPT—

   A) David Walker
   B) Rita Moreno
   C) Smokey Robinson
   D) Cesar Chavez

13. All these people were professionally involved with music or musicians EXCEPT —

   A) Berry Gordy
   B) Wallace Amos
   C) Asian American anchors
   D) Rita Moreno

14. According to the selections, all these people had to deal with prejudice and great unfairness EXCEPT —

A) Asian American anchorwomen
B) Cesar Chavez and the fruit pickers
C) David Walker
D) The Navajo Code Talkers

15. All these Americans were alive after 1900 EXCEPT —

A) Althea Gibson
B) Cesar Chavez
C) David Walker
D) Wallace Amos

13
THE BLACK ATHLETE WHO BEAT THE NAZI SUPERMEN

The Olympic Games are the greatest sports contests in the world. They are held once every four years. Athletes come to the games from all parts of the earth. Every nation sends its stars. Every country wants to be the one that has the most Olympic winners.

In 1936, the Games were held in Germany. At that time, Germany was ruled by the Nazis. The Nazi dictator, Adolf Hitler, hated all races except his own Germans. Germans, he believed, were a master race of supermen who deserved to be the rulers of the world. Hitler expected that his blond German supermen would win most of the prizes at the Games. What an upset! The star of the games was an African American. His name was Jesse Owens.

Jesse was born in Alabama in 1913. His parents were poor farm workers. As a child, Jesse was always sick. He almost died from pneumonia. He spent three winters in bed. But when skinny little Jesse was in fifth grade, his teacher saw how fast he could run. He said Jesse should try out for track. Just a few years later, in high school, Jesse Owens became famous. He broke a world record. He ran the 100-yard dash in 9.14 seconds.

Many colleges wanted Jesse. He chose Ohio State University. He was a track star there. But the day before an important track meet, he hurt his back playing touch football. The next day, he was so stiff and sore he couldn't bend over.

The 100-yard dash began. Jesse took off. He forgot everything but winning. And he won. He was so fast he tied the world record. Over the next 46 minutes, he made sports history. He won the 220-yard dash. He set a new world record. He won the 220-yard hurdles. He set a new world record. He won the long jump. He set a new world record. His long jump distance of 26 feet 8 inches wasn't beaten for another 25 years. And this was the man who couldn't bend over!

The following year was 1936—the year that the Olympic Games were held in Germany. For a while, it looked as Jesse would lose the long jump. He had three chances to qualify. The first two times, his foot was over the line when he started his jump. At least, that was what the German officials said. They said his two jumps did not count. But most people think the jumps were good, and that the officials were cheating.

PHOTOFEST

Jesse Owens, the African-American track star of the 1936 Olympic Games. Owens ran against German athletes that the Nazi leader, Adolf Hitler, said were supermen of a "Master Race." Owens beat them.

Jesse was getting really upset. He knew he was being cheated. The Germans didn't want him to jump in the Games. They were afraid that a black man would beat their supermen.

Then a German athlete walked over. He was Luz Long, the only person who had a chance to beat Jesse in the long jump. "Relax," he said. He suggested that Jesse should start his last jump a few inches early. That would make it harder for the officials to cheat. It worked. Jesse qualified and went on to win. Luz came in second. The two men became friends. They wrote to each other for many years.

Jesse won four gold medals. Besides the long jump, he came first in three other events. He won the 100-meter dash, the 200-meters dash, and the 400-meter relay race.

One hundred thousand sports fans watched Jesse receive his medals. Only one man turned his back and left the reviewing stand. It was Adolf Hitler. He said he left because of the rain. But most people think he couldn't bear to see a black man win the honors instead of his German supermen.

When Jesse returned to the States, he was greeted as a hero. New York City gave him and his teammates a giant parade. Jesse was named Athlete of the Year.

Jesse once described his running style: "I stick with the field till the last thirty yards. Then I take a big breath, hold it, tense my stomach muscles, and set sail."

Jesse Owens sailed away from the rest of the field time and again. He died in 1980, but he will be remembered as one of the greatest athletes of all time.

GLOSSARY

dash   A race in which the runners run as fast as they can for a short distance.

dictator   A ruler of a country who can do what ever he pleases.

hurdles   A race in which the runners have to jump over waist-high barriers placed on the track.

pneumonia   A serious lung disease.

EXERCISES

MATCHING

1. Put the number next to the description.

   A) He ruled Germany in 1936.
   B) He won 4 gold medals at the Olympic games.
   C) He told Jesse to try out for the school track team.
   D) He finished second in the long jump.

   1. Jesse's teacher
   2. Adolf Hitler
   3. Luz Long
   4. Jesse Owens

SEQUENCE

2. What happened last?

   A) Jesse Owens won four Olympic gold medals.
   B) Jesse Owens had a ticker tape parade.
   C) Jesse Owens caught pneumonia.
   D) Jesse Owens ran 100 yards in 9.14 seconds.

FACT/ OPINION

3. Which statement does NOT contain an opinion?

   A) Hitler hated all races except the Germans.
   B) It was raining when Hitler left the reviewing stand.
   C) Luz Long liked Jesse.
   D) Hitler didn't want a black man to win a gold medal.

FIGURATIVE LANGUAGE

4. When Jesse Owens said he set sail, he meant that—

   A) his boat moved away from the dock.
   B) he ran as fast as he could.
   C) he jumped into the air.
   D) he prayed.

MAIN IDEA

5. This selection is mainly about—

   A) one of the fastest runners of all time.
   B) the friendship between an American and a German.
   C) college sports in the 1930's.
   D) a dictator's hatred.

DRAWING CONCLUSIONS

6. In 1935 Jesse broke three world records on one day. Why was this a surprise?

   A) He was recovering from pneumonia.
   B) He kept jumping foul.
   C) He had hurt his back playing touch football.
   D) Nobody wanted him to win.

REFERENCE

7. If you wanted to find the meaning of the word *pneumonia*, what would you use?

   A) An encyclopedia
   B) An atlas
   C) A dictionary
   D) An almanac

WRITE ABOUT—

8. Imagine that you are Luz Long. Write a short paragraph in which you explain why you helped Jesse Owens qualify at Hitler's Olympics.

14
FIESTA IN
MEXICO

Everybody around the world loves a holiday. In Mexico, holidays are special times known as *fiestas*.

Fiestas have a very special place in Mexican life. The Mexican year is crowded with them. A fiesta day is filled with singing and dancing. The streets are full of brilliant colors and strange costumes. All day long, fruit, candy, and toys are sold in the markets. The night is full of songs and loud cries. Nobody talks quietly. Hats fly into the air. Laughter and curses ring out. Guitars play. The lover goes to his sweetheart's house bringing a large band along with him. Fireworks light up the skies.

Fiestas are the poor Mexican's chief luxury. They are Mexico's version of the vacation. They give all Mexicans a chance to open up. Friends who have been on polite terms suddenly become like brothers. They share their secrets and weep together over their troubles.

The fiesta is a time of joyous excess. Everyone forgets themselves. Everyone is caught up in the fiesta. All order vanishes. Anything goes. Men disguise themselves as women. The poor dress up like the rich. The rich dress like the poor. Everyone mocks the soldiers and the police. A fiesta is different from everyday life. Everything is turned upside down.

And occasionally, the happiness ends in trouble. Lovers quarrel. Friends insult each other. There are fights. But these, too are part of the fiesta. For the fiesta isn't just for fun. It's an escape. People have kept their feelings to themselves all year. Now they explode.

The Mexican fiesta even makes fun of death. Mexicans feel more comfortable with death than Europeans and Americans do. Death is not so frightening. It will come. It has to come. Death is part of life. So death is there in the fiestas, too. You can buy skulls made of sugar-candy and tissue-paper. You can see skeletons strung with fireworks. Houses are decorated with death's heads.

Some fiestas are celebrated all over the country. The whole of Mexico—from the tiniest village to the greatest city—feasts, shouts, and prays. On September 15—the day Mexico began to fight for its independence—crowds all through the country shout nonstop for a whole hour. Around December 12, everything in Mexico stops for the fiesta of the Virgin of Guadalupe. The fiesta honors the patron saint of all Mexico, the special protector of the country and its people.

There are local fiestas, too. Every city and village has its patron saint. The saint's day is a fiesta. The famous Mexican writer Octavio Paz once visited a small village. It had little money—maybe 3,000 pesos a year from taxes. Paz asked the mayor how this money was spent. The mayor replied proudly, "Mostly on fiestas, señor. We are

SEQUENCE

3. Put these events in order:

    A) James changed his name.
    B) Lafayette gave James a letter.
    C) James waited on the British general.
    D) The British general saw James in uniform.

PREDICTING OUTCOMES

4. The selection says Lafayette decided not to fight the British. Why did he decide this?

    A) He was a coward.
    B) America might win.
    C) James Armistead would die.
    D) He didn't have enought men.

SENTENCE COMPLETION

5. James Armistead was an American spy. He worked as a waiter. He listened to the British officers make plans. This way, he learned when their army _____. He sent the news back to the Americans. And so, whenever the British Army sent soldiers to a new location, the Americans already knew about it.

    A) ate
    B) moved
    C) rested
    D) surrendered

DRAWING CONCLUSIONS

6. What did Lafayette think of James Armistead?

    A) He thought that James's bravery helped win the war.
    B) He thought that James sent the wrong information.
    C) He thought that James was a good waiter.
    D) He thought that James didn't help much.

WRITE ABOUT—

7. Imagine that you are a Virginia lawmaker just after the American Revolution. You receive a copy of General Lafayette's letter. Write a very short speech in which you explain to your fellow lawmakers why you think James Armistead should be a free man.

16
THE BLIND DANCER

Beethoven wrote music when he was deaf. Alicia Alonso danced when she was almost blind. Some people love their work so much they can't stop. Alicia Alonso is one of these people.

Alicia was born in Cuba in 1921. She began to dance when she was a little girl. She wanted to learn ballet, the kind of dance that goes with classical music.

Alicia's family wasn't rich. They couldn't afford to buy special ballet shoes for her, so she danced in her sneakers. Then one day, another parent gave the class a pair of ballet shoes. Alicia's feet were the only ones to fit the shoes. Now that she had her own ballet shoes, she practiced all the time.

Alicia became Cuba's top ballet dancer. She was still only 15 years old. She wanted to dance all the time, but her father said "No!" She wanted to leave Cuba to study dance. Her father still said "No!" He expected his daughter to be a good housewife.

So Alicia ran away from home. She and her boyfriend, Fernando Alonso, went to New York. They got married. Soon they were the proud parents of a baby girl. Alicia started dance classes with new teachers as soon as she could.

The dance fans liked Alicia Alonso. When she danced, her Latin background was exciting. The dance critics loved her special flavor. Everything seemed to be going well.

Then came the shock. Alicia's eyes were going bad. The doctors had to operate. Alicia had to spend a year in bed. She couldn't see, for her eyes were bandaged. She wasn't supposed to move. Most people would give up hope of continuing a career in ballet. But Alicia found a special way to dance. She listened to the music from *Giselle*, one of the most famous and difficult of all ballets. While she listened, she practised the steps with her fingers. This was how she learned to dance the part of Giselle.

Slowly, Alicia's eyes got better. She left the hospital and looked for a job. An important dancer had just gotten sick. This dancer had the part of Giselle, the part that Alicia had danced with her fingers when she was in the hospital. The ballet company manager asked, "Has anyone here danced Giselle?" Nervously, Alicia said she had. She got the part. She danced Giselle, and she was a sensation.

Eventually, Alicia went back to Cuba and formed her own dance group. But in 1961 the United States and Cuba quarreled. For 15 years Alicia Alonso could not dance in the States. She danced all over the world with the Cuban Ballet, but not in America.

ALICIA ALONZO

Cuban ballet star Alicia Alonso. This photo was taken in the early 1950s, when Alonso was still a young woman, but she continued to dance when she was past 70.

In 1975 Alicia was allowed to dance in the States again. She was 54 years old. Most dancers retire at 40. But Alicia couldn't stop dancing. She danced at the Metropolitan Opera House in New York. The audience was full of friends and admirers. She was in tears, and so was the audience.

Alicia Alonso's eyes have gone bad again, She can hardly see at all. She is more than 70 years old. But she still dances. Her partner is her grandson. She has no plans to retire. She will dance with her great-grandson when he's ready.

GLOSSARY

housewife A married woman who does not have a paying job, but takes care of the home.

nervously. Shakily and anxiously.

audience People who watch a performance.

EXERCISES

MAIN IDEA

1. This selection tells us a lot about Alicia. Which fact is most important?

A) Alicia ran away from home.
B) Alicia has a daughter.
C) Alicia won't stop dancing.
D) Alicia married when she was very young.

FACTS/OPINIONS

2. Which is an opinion?

A) Alicia danced in New York.
B) Alicia had an eye operation.
C) Alicia was Cuba's best dancer.
D) Alicia spent a year in hospital.

CAUSE/EFFECT

3. Why did fifteen-year-old Alicia leave Cuba?

   A) She needed an eye doctor.
   B) Her boyfriend lived in New York.
   C) She wanted to learn English.
   D) She needed new dance teachers.

TRUE/FALSE

4. Which of the following does NOT describe the young Alicia Alonso?

   A) willing to take risks
   B) rich
   C) skilled
   D) hard-working

VOCABULARY DEVELOPMENT

5. When Alicia danced, her Latin background was <u>obvious</u>.

   That means:

   A) It was easy to see.
   B) It bothered people.
   C) People liked it.
   D) People hated it.

MAKING JUDGMENTS

6. What did Alicia do in the hospital?

   A) She prayed.
   B) She cried.
   C) She practiced dancing.
   D) She wrote a book.

WRITE ABOUT—

7. Suppose you were a dancer. What kind of dancing would you enjoy doing? Why do you want to do this kind of dancing?

78

17
CONCENTRATION CAMPS IN AMERICA

Life was peaceful for most Americans in 1941. Then, on December 7, Japan attacked the United States. The attack was swift. There was no warning. Suddenly Japanese planes appeared over Hawaii. They headed for ships docked at the naval base of Pearl Harbor. Hundreds of bombs fell. Every American ship was destroyed.

The United States declared war on Japan. A wave of fury at the Japanese swept over America. Soon after the attack on Pearl Harbor, President Roosevelt issued an order. It was aimed at everyone who was Japanese or Japanese-American. If they lived near the West Coast, they had to leave. If they had no place to go, they were put into concentration camps.

Americans today are ashamed about this. It was wrong to take people from their homes. It was wrong to put them into camps. Maybe there was a reason to move Japanese citizens away from the West Coast. America was fighting Japan. Some Americans believed people of Japanese descent were dangerous. They said if Japan attacked the West Coast of America, these people might side with Japan.

But many of these people were Americans. Most were not Japanese citizens. They were born in America. Americans can live where they choose. These Americans had done nothing wrong. They had committed no crimes. Yet they were rounded up and put into camps. They were denied their rights as Americans. And worse still, the Supreme Court said it was OK.

How did the government explain this? Well, it didn't, really. The army said the West Coast was a military zone. It said only certain people could live in this dangerous area. This sounds as if the army was being sensible. But it wasn't so simple.

Behind the scenes was a nasty anti-Asian racism. America was fighting Germany, too, but people of German descent weren't put into camps. The army commander, General De Witt, said, "Once a Jap, always a Jap." The government just went along with the army.

There were two kinds of Japanese, the Issei and the Nisei. The Issei were people born in Japan. Laws prevented them from becoming American citizens. The Nisei were their children. They were born in the United States and were U.S. citizens. They liked hot dogs and football games and jazz. But the army did not care if a person was an Issei or a Nisei.

Both the Issei and Nisei said they were pro-America. They wanted America to win the war. They were not pro-Japan. They were as loyal as any other group in America. There was no evidence that they were spies. Their American friends and neighbors believed they were loyal. But many Americans did not. As a Japanese minister said, "Those were really bad days fo rthe Japanesein America.

All the Japanese and Japanese-Americans were rounded up. They were put on trains and taken to camps. 120,000 people were taken to camps. Many of them sold everything they owned first. They were lucky. Most people who left things behind never saw them again.

An inmate described one of the camps. It was at Tule Lake, California. About 15,000 Nisei and Issei were taken there. It was in the middle of nowhere. The entire camp was surrounded by a wire fence. Armed soldiers patrolled outside. For three years, the people lived at Tule Lake in tar-paper shacks.

The camps were bad, but they weren't terrible. No one was beaten. People got three good meals a day. They had their own schools. They could go to church. One group—the older women—almost liked the camps. They had worked hard all their lives. They had spent their days working, cleaning, and cooking. In the camps they had plenty of free time. For them, camp life was like a vacation.

It was much harder for the older men. They couldn't provide for their families. They lost their self-respect. Families fell apart. Before the war, the Japanese family was very close. Mealtimes together were very important. But in the camps, families stopped eating together. Mothers ate with their younger children. Fathers ate with the other men. The older children ate with their friends.

After a while, people were allowed to leave the camps. Some people went to work on the farms. Some Nisei worked as translators for the army in the Pacific. After they left, the camps got worse.

GLOSSARY

concentration camps. Places where prisoners of war are kept. They are often surrounded with barbed wire, and are like a combination of an Army camp and a prison.

evidence. Facts that prove something is true.

fury. Hot anger.

naval base. A place where navy ships are kept.

patrolled. Walked around an area to guard it and to make sure no one escapes.

One surprising thing happened. The army decided to form an all-Nisei combat unit, the 442nd Regimental Combat Team. It was sent to fight Hitler in Europe. Many of the young Japanese-Americans in the camps volunteered. These young Nisei fought alongside Japanese-Americans from Hawaii. The 442nd became famous. It won more decorations than any other army unit. A movie was made about it called *Go for Broke.*

These Nisei showed they were loyal Americans. But most Japanese and Japanese-Americans weren't given this chance. They spent years behind barbed wire. They suffered because America was racist. They suffered because Americans didn't trust them.

Many years later, both California and the United States finally apologized. The people who had been in the camps were given money, and they were paid for the property that had been taken away from them.

EXERCISES

SEQUENCE

1. What happened first?

   A) The United States declared war on Japan.
   B) Japanese planes attacked the U.S..
   C) Japanese Americans were moved into camps.
   D) The 442nd Combat Team won medals.

CAUSE/ EFFECT

2. Why were people of Japanese origin put into camps?

   A) They were enemy spies.
   B) Americans didn't want them to mix with Germans.
   C) Racial prejudice made Americans distrust them.
   D) They wanted to quit work for a while.

MAKING JUDGMENTS

3. Who was happiest in the camps?

   A) children
   B) young men and women
   C) older men
   D) older women

MAKING JUDGMENTS

4. All the following thought the Japanese should leave the West Coast, EXCEPT—

   A) the Issei and Nisei.
   B) the Army.
   C) the Supreme Court.
   D) the government.

COMPARE/ CONTRAST

5. How did the Nisei differ from the Issei?

   A) The Nisei had Japanese parents.
   B) The Nisei were born in America.
   C) The Nisei were born in Japan.
   D) The Nisei had American parents.

CAUSE/ EFFECT

6. Why are people today ashamed that Issei and Nissei were sent to concentration camps?

   A) American citizens were deprived of their rights.
   B) People in the camps were treated brutally.
   C) These camps encouraged anti-American feeling.
   D) Children in the camps got no schooling.

REFERENCE

7. If you wanted to find out where Tule Lake is, what would you use?

   A) A telephone directory
   B) An atlas
   C) A dictionary
   D) An almanac

8. You are a young Nisei who has just been let out of the Tule Lake Camp. An army sergeant asks you if you would be willing to join an all-Nisei combat unit that will fight the Nazis in Europe. Write a few sentences telling what your answer is, and giving your reasons.

18
REVIEW QUESTIONS

I. CROSSWORD

CLUES ACROSS

1. Mexican feast day.
3. In the 1936 _____Games, an American won three gold medals.
5. Sugar candy skulls remind Mexicans of this.
7. Name given to Japanese living in America but born in Japan.

CLUES DOWN

2. James Armistead was one.
3. America's fastest runner for many years.
4. Alicia Alonso was born here.
6. Alicia danced on this part of her foot a lot.

II. MISSING PERSONS

In each of these passages, a person's <u>last</u> name is hidden. The passage also gives a clue about the hidden person.

8. How warm is tea drunk here? Very warm indeed. Serve it piping hot to the British officers, young man.

9. Going slow ensures losing the race. I never lose.

10. You can dance a good deal on some stages. Others wear out very quickly.

III. MATCHING

After the name of each person below, put the letter of the place and the event that goes with the person. Choose 1 place and 1 event for each person.

PLACE

    A) a British army camp
    B) Ohio State University
    C) a hospital

EVENT

    X) learns about British plans
    Y) dances *Giselle* using fingers
    Z) breaks four world records

11. Jesse Owens   _____   _____

12. Alicia Alonso   _____   _____

13. James Armistead   _____   _____

19
KING OF SALSA

Rubén Blades is a singer and a songwriter. He is a popular performer of the popular Hispanic-American music called *salsa*. Salsa is a spicy, hot sauce. Salsa music has a hot, spicy Latino beat. Blades' songs have the salsa beat that makes them great for dancing. But what makes his songs really special is the words. When Blades writes a song, he doesn't write what he calls "mira-mira-let's-dance-baby-let's-dance." His songs are about people. Real people. About the problems they face. About their struggle to be decent human beings.

Rubén Blades was born in Panama. His father was a policeman. His mother acted in radio soap operas. As a child, he loved all things American. He and his friends liked American pop music. They listened to it all the time on the radio. Soon they began singing doo-wop. They looked for places with an echo. The echo made them sound as if they were on the radio. They always sang in English.

In 1963, things changed. There was a bloody riot in Panama. A law said that some buildings must fly two flags—Panama's flag and the U.S. Stars and Stripes. Americans refused to fly the Panamanian flag. A riot broke out. Twenty-one people were killed and five hundred wounded.

Blades blamed America. He stopped singing in English and threw himself into Latin music. In the 1960's, he played with many Latin bands.

But Blades had many other interests besides music. He wanted an education. He got a law degree from the University of Panama. He worked as a lawyer for a while. Then he went back to music.

Then in the 1970's, Blades moved to New York. In 1976 he wrote songs for Willie Colón's Combo. He began to sing, too. People listened to these new songs. The words were serious. They were often on political subjects.

One of Blades' most famous songs was "Tiburón." This means "The Shark." In this song, Blades showed his anger at the way the United States was treating Central American nations. The shark in the song was the United States. This song was banned on Miami's most popular Latin-music radio station.

In the 1980's, Blades formed his own band. He began to record for Elektra, a big recording company. His first record was *Buscando America* ("Looking for America"). It was very popular. The critics loved it. *Buscando America* sold over 300,00 copies. Many of the songs on this record were political, too. One song was about a Central American priest gunned down in his own church. Another describes a day in the life of a secret policeman.

RUBÉN BLADES

Rubén Blades—songwriter, musician, actor, lawyer, and politician—a man who seems able to do anything.

Blades still sings. But he does a lot of other things as well. He took time off from music again in 1985. He went to Harvard University to study more about the law. He is an actor. He starred in *Crossover Dreams*, a movie about a Latin singer who wanted to appeal to Anglos. He played a laid-back, peace-loving New Mexico sheriff in Robert Redford's movie *The Milagro Beanfield Wars.* He writes about politics for a newspaper in Panama.

He's interested in music. He's interested in politics. He's interested in law. He's interested in movie-making. No one knows what he will do next.

GLOSSARY

mira   Spanish for "Look!" or "Hey!"

decent   Honest and not harming or bothering anyone.

doo-wop   A pop music sound of the early 1960's. Doo-wop usually featured a lead singer backed by a group singing rhythm words that sounded like "doo-wop, doo-wop."

echo   Sound bouncing back off a hard object.

banned   Not allowed.

EXERCISES

COMPARE/CONTRAST

1. According to the selection, what makes Blades' songs different from other salsa songs?

    A) They're good to dance to.
    B) The words are silly.
    C) They're about real people and real issues.
    D) They're all written in English.

WORD MEANINGS

2. In *Crossover Dreams*, Blades played a Latino singer who wanted to <u>appeal to</u> non-Latinos. Which words have the same meaning as "appeal to"?

    A) ask about
    B) beg for
    C) work out
    D) be liked by

MAKING JUDGMENTS

3. Why did Blades stop singing in English?

    A) He blamed the United States for the riot in Panama.
    B) He stopped liking doo-wop songs.
    C) He decided Latino music was better.
    D) He wanted to go to law school.

FIGURATIVE LANGUAGE

4. In the song "Tiburón" the United States is compared to:

    A) Central America
    B) a shark
    C) the victim of a shark
    D) Panama

FACTS/OPINIONS

2. Which statement is a fact, not an opinion?

   A) Hirrihigua was a cruel man.
   B) Juan was a gentle person.
   C) Hirrihigua was wrong to kill the Spanish soldiers.
   D) Juan was captured by the Indians.

VOCABULARY DEVELOPMENT

3. The chief's wife treated Juan with <u>herbs</u>.

   That means—

   A) prayers
   B) special plants
   C) hot sand
   D) kindness

CAUSE/EFFECT

4. Why did the Spanish soldiers become friends with Mucozo?

   A) He fought against Hirrihigua.
   B) He spoke Spanish.
   C) He was kind to Juan.
   D) He loved Hirrihigua's daughter.

REFERENCE

5. Spanish soldiers came to Florida from Seville.

   Suppose you wanted to see how far they had traveled. Where would you get this information?

   A) a dictionary
   B) the *Readers' Guide to Periodical Literature*
   C) a thesaurus
   D) an atlas

PREDICTING OUTCOMES

6. What do you think happened to Juan?

   A) He stayed with the Spanish army
   B) He went back to Hirrihigua
   C) He fought against Mucozo
   D) He fought against the Spanish army

WRITE ABOUT—

7. Suppose you are Chief Mucozo. You are protecting Juan Ortiz. A messenger comes from Chief Hirrihigua. Hirrihigua demands that Juan be returned to him. What would you tell the messenger? What reasons would you give for refusing to return Juan?

21
EL BARRIO

In Spanish, a *barrio* is a city neighborhood. Many Spanish speakers call their neighborhoods "barrios." There are many barrios in the cities of the United States.

Sometimes, the people who live in a barrio are poor. One famous, dirt-poor barrio in San Jose, California, is called Sal Si Puedes. This means "Get out if you can!" It was home to the famous labor leaders Cesar and Helen Chavez for many years. Other famous barrios are in East Los Angeles. The well-known actor Edward James Olmos grew up there.

The most famous barrio in New York is just called El Barrio. It's located uptown on Manhattan island. To the people who live there, El Barrio is special.

El Barrio is home to many poor people. Its streets are filled with old buildings. They're overcrowded. Sometimes they're dirty. Some people call it a slum. But it is full of life. It's a distinctly Puerto Rican life. Movie-houses show Spanish-language films. Travel agencies offer cheap flights to Puerto Rico. Jukeboxes play Spanish records. There are Latino restaurants and bakeries. Everything has a Spanish flavor—laundries and dance halls, bars and *bodegas*. A bodega is a small grocery store. Many of its goods come from Puerto Rico and its neighbor islands.

El Barrio is full of small churches. They are sandwiched between the stores. Most Puerto Ricans were Catholics when they lived in Puerto Rico. Many changed when they came to New York. These people now go to Baptist Churches or Pentecostal Churches. Church services are often lively. People sing and clap. Churches also serve as social centers. They run athletic clubs and other kinds of clubs.

In winter, the streets are empty. People stay indoors. But in summer, El Barrio comes alive. The streets are humming. Puerto Rico is a warm island. People spend a lot of time outdoors. So in the hot New York summer, people go outside, too. Puerto Ricans spend most of their free time outdoors. The air fills with Latino music. People gather in front of their buildings for meetings and sidewalk parties. Children play stickball. Young people go dancing. Weddings move noisily through the streets.

El Barrio can be colorful and exciting. It's nearly always friendly. Often, neighbors form lifetime friendships. They share what little they have. Doors are open to hungry children and adults. This warmth is strongest within the family. Some families have fallen apart. But most families that came from the island have stayed together.

Puerto Ricans have another way of enjoying themselves in the summer. They build little houses on vacant lots. The houses are called *casitas*. They're made with materials found on the streets. Most casitas are painted sky blue. People use them as club houses. They grow things outside. You can find okra, tomatoes, cabbage, squash, cucumbers, and eggplant. Some casita gardens even have peach trees, apple trees, and strawberry beds. The owners also keep animals. In El Barrio's casitas you can find ducks, chicken, geese, even a peacock.

Some casitas are quite fancy. They have sun decks on the roofs. Down below you can find a refrigerator, a charcoal cooker, and some old furniture. It's easy to imagine you're in a small cottage on a back country road. It doesn't feel like New York City.

Life has not been easy for Puerto Ricans who came from the island. They came to find jobs. The jobs they found often paid little. But at least they had work. The tenements are often cold and dark. But they are home. It can be tough on the mainland. But friends and families make life in El Barrio a lot easier.

GLOSSARY

dirt-poor   Very poor.

stickball   A street version of baseball.

tenements   Poor, run-down apartment houses.

98

EXERCISES

MAIN IDEA

1. This selection is about—

    A) life in New York's El Barrio.
    B) casitas.
    C) tenement buildings.
    D) North American barrios.

DRAWING CONCLUSIONS

2. You can find all these things in El Barrio, EXCEPT:

    A) apple trees.
    B) Baptist churches.
    C) Spanish-language movies.
    D) large wild animals.

IDIOM

3. The author says that some families have <u>fallen apart</u>. This means some families have—

    A) left New York.
    B) borrowed a lot of money.
    C) split up.
    D) lost everything.

WORD MEANING

4. What is a <u>casita</u>?

    A) a video store that sells Spanish-language videos
    B) a small home-made house and garden
    C) a place where you can dance
    D) a church

CHARACTERS' MOTIVATION

5. Why do people build casitas?

    A) To do their grocery shopping
    B) To brighten up their lives
    C) To find jobs
    D) To pray on Sundays

REFERENCE

6. If you wanted to find New York City, San Jose, or Los Angeles on a map, what book would you use?

    A) an atlas
    B) an encyclopedia
    C) an almanac
    D) a dictionary

WRITE ABOUT—

7. Suppose you live in El Barrio in New York City. You are planning a casita in a lot near you. What will it be like? What color will you paint it, and what will you grow near it?

22
THE GREAT MOCTEZUMA

Bernal Díaz del Castillo was a young soldier in the Spanish army that destroyed the kingdom of the Aztecs. When he was an old man, he wrote about his adventures and about the marvelous things he saw. This is his description of the the king of the Aztecs, the Great Moctezuma (sometimes called Montezuma). It also is one of the first descriptions of a delicious Aztec food that was new to Europeans—chocolate.

The Great Moctezuma was about forty years old. He was of good height and well-built, slender and without any extra fat. He was not very dark-skinned, but of the natural color and shade of an Indian. He did not wear his hair long, but so as to just cover his ears. His black beard was well-shaped but thin. His face was somewhat long but cheerful. In his appearance and manner he showed both tenderness and, when necessary, seriousness. He was very neat and clean and bathed once a day in the afternoon. The clothes that he wore one day, he did not put on again until four days later.

He had over two hundred chiefs as guards in rooms close to his own. When they went to speak to him, they had to take off their rich cloaks and put on poor ones. They had to enter barefoot with their eyes lowered to the ground, and not look up into his face. They had to bow three times, and say, "Lord, my Lord, my Great Lord," before they came up to him. When they left, they did not turn their backs, but kept their faces towards him with their eyes on the ground. They did not turn their backs until they left the room.

I noticed another thing—that when other great chiefs came from far away to speak to him, they had to come barefoot and with poor cloaks. They were not allowed to come right into the palace, but had to wait a while at one side of the palace door. To go right in without waiting was thought to be disrespectful.

For each meal that the Great Moctezuma ate, over thirty dishes were prepared. His cooks placed small pottery heaters below the dishes so they would not get cold. Every day they cooked chickens, turkeys, pheasants, native partridges, tame and wild ducks, deer, wild pigs, pigeons, rabbits, and other things that are found in that country. There were so many different things that I cannot finish naming them in a hurry. The cooks prepared more than three hundred plates of the food that Moctezuma was going to eat.

MICHAEL M^cDERMOTT

Moctezuma, ruler of the Aztec nation. No truly accurate portrait of him exists. This picture is based on eyewitness descriptions and on drawings made by Aztec artists after he was dead.

This is the way things were served to him at mealtime. He sat on a low stool, soft and richly decorated. The table, which was low, was made in the same style as the seats. On it they placed table cloths of white cloth and some rather long napkins of the same material.

Four very beautiful women brought water for his hands in a deep gourd, and they held other gourds below to catch the water, and they brought him towels. And two other women brought him tortilla bread. And as soon as he began to eat, they placed before him a sort of wooden screen painted over with gold so that no one could watch him eating. While he was at his meal, the men of his guard who were in nearby rooms never dreamed of making any noise or speaking aloud.

They brought him fruit of all the different kinds that the land produced, but he ate very little of it. From time to time they brought him, in cups of pure gold, a certain drink made from chocolate, and the women served this drink to him with great reverence.

GLOSSARY

barefoot Without shoes.

cloaks Long pieces of cloth that cover the shoulders and back.

disrespectful Rude.

gourd A vegetable like a squash, which is often dried and hollowed out for use as a bowl.

reverence Deep respect.

tortilla bread A flat round bread made from corn flour.

EXERCISES

AUTHOR'S VIEWPOINT

1. What is the author's attitude towards Moctezuma?

    A) respect mixed with amazement
    B) dislike mixed with fear
    C) friendliness
    D) amusement

PURPOSE OF SELECTION

2. Why does the author spend so much time describing Moctezuma's meal?

    A) to show his readers how the Aztecs cooked
    B) to make his readers feel hungry
    C) to show how rich and powerful Moctezuma was
    D) to make his readers laugh

MAKING JUDGMENTS

3. Why did other chiefs wear poor cloaks when they came before Moctezuma?

    A) because they were poor themselves
    B) because they ruled over poor people
    C) because they didn't know how to make rich cloaks
    D) because their clothing had to show that they ranked far below Moctezuma

SUPPORTING DETAILS

4. What was the screen for?

    A) to hide Moctezuma when he was changing his clothes
    B) to keep people from seeing Moctezuma eating
    C) to prevent people from seeing Moctezuma's guards
    D) to keep out the wind

PREDICTING OUTCOMES

5. Suppose a chief was visiting Moctezuma. When it was time to leave, he bowed, turned around, and started to walk out. What do you think Moctezuma would probably do?

   A) have the chief punished for not backing out of the room
   B) call goodbye to him
   C) walk politely to the door with him
   D) call the next chief in

WRITE ABOUT—

6. Many Aztec customs were invented to show how great the king was. Suppose that Moctezuma wanted to invent a new custom to show how great he was. He asks you for advice. What custom would you suggest?

23
THE BEAUTY BUSINESS OF MADAME C. J. WALKER

Madame C.J. Walker was the first African-American woman to become a millionaire. Her company made beauty aids—make-up, shampoos, skin creams—for African-American women. She was very successful. She made as much money as Elizabeth Arden and Helena Rubinstein, whose companies made cosmetics for white women.

Madame Walker was born Sarah Breedlove in Louisiana in 1867. Her parents were poor farmers. Both of them died when Sarah was still a child. She married when she was 14, but her husband died six years later. For the next ten years, Sarah made her living by washing clothes. She only made $1.50 a day. But she was ambitious. She wanted to be a success.

Sarah studied new ways to style hair. She had lots of different ideas. In 1905, she came up with a new hair treatment for African-American women. She tried it out on her friends. First, she used a special shampoo. It had a new kind of cream. Then she applied heated iron combs. Finally, she brushed the hair hard. It worked. Her friends loved the way their hair looked. Sarah opened her own business.

In 1906, she married again. Her second husband was named Charles J. Walker, and so Sarah called herself Madame C.J. Walker. Meanwhile, her business grew larger. She hired more people. Her employees worked hard. They went to people's homes with her hair products. Women loved the new look. Soon the Walker Beauty Care System was famous throughout the United States. It was popular in Jamaica. Walker products even reached Europe. In Paris, the great singer and dancer, Josephine Baker, used Sarah's shampoo.

In 1913, Madame Walker moved to New York City. Walker Beauty Salons opened all over the city. Madame Walker started a college to train young women in how to give the Walker Beauty Treatment.

Madame Walker became rich. She built a big house in Harlem and gave big parties. Famous African-American writers and musicians visited her. She also owned a mansion next to the Hudson River. She could easily afford both homes. The Walker Manufacturing Company was the largest and most successful black-owned business in America.

Sarah Walker was not stingy. She wanted to help other African Americans, and she was generous with her money. She gave huge sums to the NAACP. She also helped her employees. People who worked for her led good lives. Her employees, in turn, helped their communities. People who worked for Madame Walker were respected. Her company had the highest reputation.

Madame C.J. Walker was a great American entrepreneur. She was rich and powerful. But she also worked hard for others.

GLOSSARY

ambitious Eager to get ahead and be successful.

cosmetics Beauty aids, like face powder, lipstick, etc.

mansion A huge house.

NAACP An organization that works for the interests and benefits of African Americans.

EXERCISES

MAIN IDEA

1. What was Madame Walker's beauty business?

   A) running beauty salons
   B) manufacturing and selling beauty products
   C) judging beauty contests
   D) photographing beautiful women

SEQUENCE

2. Which happened first?

   A) Sarah married C.J. Walker.
   B) Sarah had large parties.
   C) Sarah gave money to the NAACP.
   D) Sarah helped Josephine Baker.

CONTEXT CLUES

3. The last paragraph of the selection calls Madame Walker a great <u>entrepreneur</u>. An entrepreneur is someone who—

   A) steals money.
   B) starts a business.
   C) travels a lot.
   D) exercises a lot.

SUPPORTING DETAILS

4. What was Madame Walker's first success?

   A) a hair treatment
   B) a new lipstick
   C) a new face powder
   D) a treatment for broken nails

PREDICTING OUTCOMES

5. Suppose Madame Walker wanted to expand her business to another continent.

   Which continent would be best for her business?

   A) Africa
   B) Asia
   C) Australia
   D) Antarctica

WRITE ABOUT—

6. Women are becoming more and more involved in businesses. Write a few sentences about any woman you know or have heard about who works in a business or who has her own business. Describe what this woman does.

24
REVIEW QUESTIONS

I. MAP

Here is a map of Central America and the Caribbean. There are four places marked on the map. Each place is connected with someone in the selections you've just read. Match the person or people with the place.

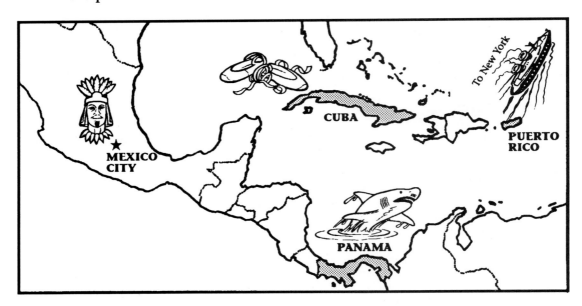

1. PANAMA

   A) Alicia Alonso
   B) Moctezuma
   C) Madame C. J. Walker
   D) Rubén Blades

2. PUERTO RICO

   A) People who came to El Barrio
   B) Moctezuma's guards
   C) Rubén Blades
   D) Chief Hirrihigua and his people

3. MEXICO CITY

   A) Rubén Blades
   B) Juan Ortiz
   C) The Great Moctezuma
   D) People who came to El Barrio

4. CUBA

   A) Alicia Alonso
   B) Rubén Blades
   C) Madame C. J. Walker
   D) The Aztecs

5. "Doo woppa doo woppa doo woppa doo."

   "Oh, the shark. He is a thief, a thief."

   "Yes, I have many interests. Music, law, politics. . ."

   A) Alicia Alonso
   B) Madame C. J. Walker
   C) Ruben Bladés
   D) Mexicans at a fiesta

6. "I have 300 dishes served to me at every meal."

   "How dare anyone talk when I am eating?"

   "Ah! It is afternoon. Time for my bath."

   A) Ruben Bladés
   B) Moctezuma
   C) Chief Hirrihigua
   D) Chief Mucozo

7. "Seville, Seville, Seville."

   "I'm so tired, I can't run any more."

   "Don't be afraid. I shall tell the soldiers what you have done for me."

   A) Rubén Blades
   B) Juan Ortiz
   C) Chief Hirrihigua
   D) Moctezuma

8. "I should never have played touch football yesterday."

   "Thanks, my friend. I see there are some good people in your country."

   "Then I take a big breath. Hold it and set sail."

   A) James Armistead
   B) Juan Ortiz
   C) Jesse Owens
   D) Alicia Alonso

III. WHO WORE IT?

9. Match the clothes with the wearer. Put the correct letter in the blanks.

A) toe shoes and a ballet dancer's skirt

B) an undershirt and running shorts

C) a fine military coat from the American Revolution

D) native American clothes

1. ____ James Armistead

2. ____ Juan Ortiz

3. ____ Jesse Owens

4. ____ Alicia Alonso

IV. THE WRONG WORD

In each of these passages, one word is not true or incorrect.
Find the word and underline it.

10. Madame C.J. Walker founded her own business. She and her assistants helped men with their hair. In time, Madame Walker became rich and famous.

11. Nisei and Issei living on the East Coast were rounded up. Then they were taken to concentration camps.

12. El Barrio is full of people from Puerto Rico. In winter, the streets are crowded and many people build casitas.

13. The Great Moctezuma wore his hair long enough to cover his ears. He was richly dressed and very dirty.

112